CHINESE COOKING
RESTAURANT STYLE

COMPILED BY LILY GER

HEIAN

序

By Lily Ger

Photos by Leu Tian-der
Book Design by Yvone Wang and ChenJau-yeuan
Executive: George Kuei

First American Edition 1994

HEIAN INTERNATIONAL, INC.
Publishers
1815 W. 205th St. Ste# 301
Torrance, CA 90501

94 95 96 97 98 99 00 10 9 8 7 6 5 4 3 2 1

ISBN: 0-89346-797-9

Printed in Hong Kong

When I was young, my favorite place in the house was the kitchen. It was there that I watched my mother prepare the meals that filled not only our stomachs but our hearts. My mother told me that food prepared with love would always be tasty.

Now that I am an adult and have entered the restaurant trade, I have had the opportunity to taste delicacies of all kinds. I have been lucky enough to have studied cooking techniques with a number of master chefs, and I am especially indebted to my mentor, Lian Zhiheng, for teaching me that a kind heart, plus technique and experience, will result in well-presented and delicious cuisine.

This book thus presents the accumulated wisdom of a number of chefs presently active in Taiwan. I hope that you, the reader, will take and adapt those methods and recipes that will enable you to create delicious and memorable meals for your family.

Lily Ger, Author and Editor

CONTENTS

CUTTING TECHNIQUES

Chinese cuisine aims for perfection and balance among three elements in each dish-- color, fragrance, and flavor. Cutting is one of the most important factors that influences the taste of a dish. Ingredients that should be cubed cannot be cut into slices; those that should be sliced thinly should not be sliced thickly. In a restaurant, the person who is in charge of cutting ingredients is very important--almost every chef in a big restaurant was first responsible for cutting ingredients. Chef Liang Zhiheng here illustrates several cutting techniques.

■ Pork Tenderloin

This is the most commonly used cut of meat; it can be shredded, sliced, cubed or sliced thickly as for pork chops. No matter how it is used, the tenderloin should first be prepared by removing its membrane and sinews. These elements make the meat difficult to cut and change the flavor of the meat as well. For tender stir-fried pork, it is important to always cut against the grain. Should very thin slices be required, it is sometimes better to place the meat in the freezer for a short while; partially frozen meat is easier to slice thinly.

1. Remove membrane.

2. Remove sinews.

3. Slice pork tenderloin.

4. Cut meat into slivers against the grain after slicing.

5. Thick chunk slicing

6. Cubing chunks

■ Kidneys

The Chinese consider kidney meat to be a tonic for pregnant women, the sick and the weak; it is also a popular item for home cooking.

Kidneys contain a number of white sinews--these must be removed before cooking or they impart an undesirable odor to the food. A decorative pattern scored into the surface of the kidneys can add to the visual appreciation of a dish.

1. Slice kidney open horizontally.

2. White sinews become visible.

3. Remove white sinews with cleaver or cutting knife.

4. Slash the surface diagonally.

5. Score to create rhombus shape.

6. Cut into chunks.

7. Press meat down with hand to guide knife through kidney.

■ Beef Tenderloin

Beef tenderloin is almost as popular in Chinese cooking as pork tenderloin. It is handled in much the same way.

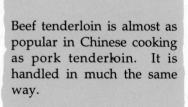

1. Slice thinly.

2. Cut slices against the grain for shredded beef.

■ Chicken

Chicken is a popular food--not only is it nutritious, it also has less cholesterol content than either pork or beef. It is a very versatile meat.

Thighs, wings, breasts and drumsticks can all be used in a number of different dishes, and the thighs and wings are perhaps more versatile than the other parts. Chicken may be roasted, broiled, fried, steamed or stewed--any method can result in a delicious dish. Bones, claws and head can even be used for soup--thus, the entire chicken can be used for a wide range of dishes.

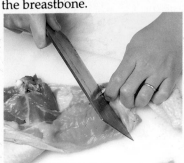

1. Remove feet at joint.

2. Cut off head.

3. Cut skin along backbone.

4. Cut along both sides of the breastbone.

5. Cut open from neck to breast.

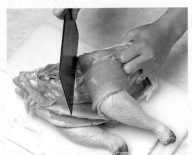

6. Using hand and cleaver to assist, pull away breast, wing and thigh from breast cage.

7. Cut off wings.

8. Cut inside of wing.

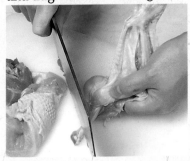

9. Remove bones through cut made.

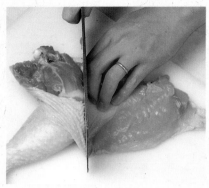

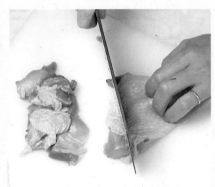

10. Cut off breast meat.

11. Cut breast meat into chunks.

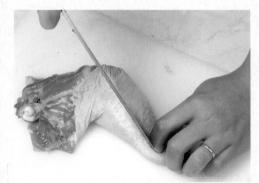

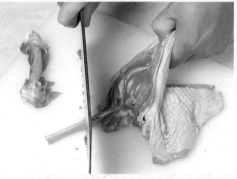

12. Cut through skin along leg bones.

13. Remove drumstick bone through cut made.

14. Remove thigh bone.

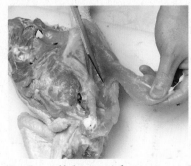

15. Cut off drumstick meat.

16. Cut drumstick meat into slices.

17. Slice drumstick meat into slivers.

■ Fish

There are innumerable varieties of edible fish; some are suitable for steaming, some for frying, some for braising and some for deep-frying.

Here we will illustrate cutting techniques using a carp. This fish has already been scaled and gutted prior to cutting. Carp can be steamed, used for soup or fried.

1. Cut behind the anterior fin near the gill.

2. Cut open along spine.

3. Continue cutting down the spine, removing meat from the bone.

4. Cut across original cut by fin, continuing to remove meat from bone.

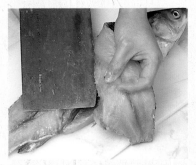

5. Continue to fillet, removing meat from bones.

6. Cut off stomach meat.

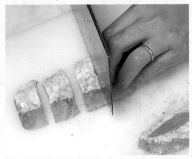

7. Cut stomach meat into chunks.

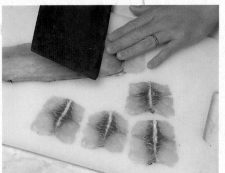

8. Fillet sliced as thin as possible.

9. Fillet sliced into thick slices.

Above are a few dishes that require the use of fish cutting techniques.

■ Shrimp

Shrimp are easy to handle. Generally, the heads are removed, the body shelled and deveined. A slash along the central back spine will cause shrimps to roll up into a circular shape when cooked.

Shrimp "steaks" can also be prepared by slashing lightly along the back of the butterflied shrimp and flattening the shrimp with a cleaver.

1. Remove head; shell shrimp but leave tail shell attached.

2. Cut along spine of shrimp to make shrimp roll up when cooked.

3. Devein shrimp.

4. Flatten with cleaver into "steak."

■ Crab

Crabs should be purchased live. Dead crabs quickly become home to breeding bacteria and can be unsafe to eat.

Crab may be prepared in a variety of ways. Here are some various cutting guidelines to be followed for all types of crabs.

1. Cut crab along belly (underside of shell).

2. Open crab, removing bottom shell.

3. Clean, removing gills.

4. Cut off claws.

5. Cut off tips of claws.

6. Cut crab into four chunks.

7. Cut at claw joint.

8. Using cleaver, break shell.

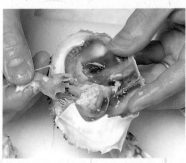

9. Clean out unwanted innards.

■ Squid

There are three kinds of squid available on the market--fresh, dried, and water-soaked. Dried squid keeps for a long time; it can be roasted or cooked after soaking in water.

If fresh or water-soaked squid is yellowish and soft to the touch, it should be avoided.

1. Remove "rib" of squid.

2. Slice meat diagonally.

3. Cut squid body in half.

4. Cut into rhombus-shaped pieces.

5. Cut tail into strips.

■ Abalone

Abalone is quite expensive and in its fresh form difficult to handle. As a consequence, one generally eats it at restaurants.

If you want to try cooking abalone at home, it is perhaps best to use canned abalone (although fresh abalone is tastier.). The meat can be sliced and used in soups or braised.

1. Cutting the abalone.

13

■ Scallions

Scallions help to dispel odors and enhance the flavors of dishes. They are inexpensive and extremely versatile.

They can be chopped, cut into sections or shredded.

1. Cutting scallions into sections.

2. Cutting sections in half lengthwise.

3. Shredding scallion sections.

4. Cutting diagonally into 2" long sections.

5. Chopping scallions.

■ Green Peppers

Green peppers, whether long and smooth or rounded and lantern-shaped, impart wonderful fragrance and flavor to dishes in which they are used.

When stir-frying, do not overcook green pepper; it becomes soft and bitter.

1. Cut off stem end.

2. Cut open; remove seeds and inner membranes.

3. Slice or cut into rhombus shape.

4. Cutting into long, thin strips.

■ Red Chiles

Natives of Szechwan and Hunan love hot chiles; they even put them in their soup! The hottest part of the chile is the seed; remove the seeds before cutting into shreds or chunks for cooking.

If your hands become hot as a result of working with the chiles, soak your hands in warm water for a short while.

1. Cut off stem end; cut open lengthwise.

2. Remove seeds.

3. Shredding chile pepper.

4. Cutting chile pepper in rhombus shapes.

■ Carrots

Nutritious and full of Vitamin A, C, and sodium, carrots are of great benefit to one's health. They may be cut into chunks, sliced or shredded.

Carrot juice can also be made; adding lemon juice and honey makes it very tasty and a good aid to digestion.

1. Carrots cut into rhombus shaped chunks.

2. Carrots cut into patterned shapes.

3. Slicing carrots.

4. Shredding carrots.

GARNISHES

Preparation is very important in Chinese cooking. Whether a beautiful butterfly, a lovely tomato basket or lifelike dragons and phoenixes--all can add a finishing touch to an interesting dish, creating a visual as well as delicious feast.

Master Chef Liang here demonstrates a few simple decorative touches for all occasions.

■ Cucumber

The bright green of the cucumber skin and its white flesh make a pleasant contrast. It will retain its color for a long time as well.

1. Cut cucumber in half.

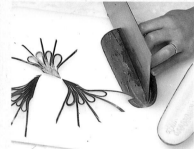

2. Cut half in half again.

3. Remove pulp.

4. Slice obliquely into thin slices.

5. Make butterfly as illustrated.

■ Carrots

Soak carrot in salted water until it is softened; it is easier to cut the carrot into sections and engrave designs. One may use a cleaver and a small fruit knife as well.

While some restaurants dye carrots, they are generally colorful to use as is.

1. Cut carrot into 2" sections; cut exterior into sawtooth pattern.

2. Slice thinly.

3. Fold the thin slices.

4. Affix folded carrot with toothpicks as shown.

■ Eggplant

The deep purple color of the eggplant makes the eggplant flower especially appealing.

1. Cut off stem end; cut into 2" sections.

2. Cut 5 slashes lengthwise for each section.

3. Cut out triangular pieces on one end, as illustrated.

4. Cut away skin from insides; remove insides and replace with a maraschino cherry.

17

■ Red Chile Pepper

"Chile flowers" can easily be made from red chile peppers.

1. Cut off one end, leaving stem-end intact.

2. Slice open chile, forming several strips around the chile

3. Using scissors, cut the tip of the each strip so that it comes to a point. Soak in cold water; "petals" will open and curl. Drain and use as garnish.

■ Scallions and Red Chile Peppers

These garnishes are easy to create and look especially attractive with meat dishes.

1. Cut scallions into sections; cut red chiles crosswise to create circles.

2. Put scallion section into chile circle.

3. Shred scallion lengthwise; soak in water so scallion shreds curl. Remove, drain and use.

■ Tomato

Two methods of making tomato "flowers" are introduced here. Green tomatoes work better than red for creating these garnishes.

1. Cut tomato into four parts.

1. Make diagonal cuts symmetrically as shown.

2. Hollow out two of the skins.

2. Cut the symmetrically cut area in half as shown.

3. Arrange pieces as shown, placing marachino cherry in middle.

3. Return the cut area to the top of the tomato, fan out the pieces attractively and place a maraschino cherry in the middle.

Braised Curried Spareribs

Ingredients:

1 lb. spareribs, cut into 1" lengths

2 onions

2 t. curry powder

Flour

1 t. salt

1 t. sugar

1 1/2 T. soy sauce

1 1/2 T. rice wine

Instructions:

1. Peel and slice onion. Marinate spareribs in 1 T. soy sauce, 1 t. curry powder, and 1/2 T. rice wine. Dredge in flower.

2. Heat oil in wok; when hot, deep fry spareribs for 5 minutes. Remove and drain well. Reheat oil; fry spareribs again for 1-2 minutes; remove and drain.

3. Remove all oil save 2 T.; heat. Fry onions till soft, then add 1/2 T. soy sauce, 1 t. salt, sugar and curry powder together with 1/2 C. water. Bring to boil; add spareribs.

4. Braise until spareribs are tender and flavors mixed. Remove and serve hot.

Braised Spareribs and Bitter Melon

Ingredients:

1 lb. spareribs, cut in 1" lengths

8 oz. bitter melon

1/2 T. fermented and salted soy beans

2 slices of ginger

1 T. chopped scallions

1 t. salt

1 t. sugar

1 1/2 T. soy sauce

1/2 T. rice wine

Instructions:

1. Marinate spareribs in 1 T. rice wine, minced ginger and soy sauce. Cut open bitter melon; remove seeds and cut into bite-sized sections.

2. Heat 3 T. oil in wok. When oil is hot, stir-fry scallions, ginger slices and fermented soy beans until fragrant. Add bitter melon pieces and stir-fry briefly.

3. Add 2 C. water, 1 T. soy sauce and simmer for 20 minutes.

4. When bitter melon is tender, add salt and sugar. Increase heat to reduce liquid; serve hot.

Shredded Pork and Bean Sprouts

Ingredients:

8 oz. bean sprouts

1 lb. boneless pork loin

1 T. chopped scallions

1 t. salt

1 t. sugar

1 1/2 T. soy sauce

1 T. rice wine

Cornstarch

Instructions:

1. Shred pork, mix well with 1 T. soy sauce, chopped scallions, rice wine and small amount cornstarch. Remove stem of bean sprouts.

2. Heat 3 T. oil in wok. When hot, stir-fry bean sprouts briefly. Remove. Re-heat oil, stir-fry pork until color changes. Add bean sprouts, stir-fry to mix well; add salt, sugar, and 1/2 T. soy sauce. Combine all ingredients and serve hot.

Shredded Pork with Bean Thread Noodles

Ingredients:

1 lb. boneless pork loin

Several tree ear fungi and water chestnuts

1 bundle bean thread noodles

1/2 T. garlic, minced

1 T. chopped scallions

1/2 T. ginger, minced

1/2 T. hot bean sauce

1/2 T. vinegar

1/2 t. salt

1 1/2 T. soy sauce

Cornstarch

1 t. sugar

Instructions:

1. Shred pork; marinate with 1 T. soy sauce and a small amount of cornstarch.
2. Shred fungi; chop water chestnuts; soak bean thread noodles to soften.
3. Heat 4 T. oil in wok; when hot, stir-fry pork until color changes. Remove and drain.
4. Re-heat oil; stir-fry ginger, garlic, scallions and bean sauce until fragrant. Add fungi, water chestnuts and pork; continue to stir-fry. Season with sugar and vinegar, then thicken with cornstarch/water solution.
5. Place drained noodles in casserole; add 1/2 C. water, 1/2 t. salt and 1/2 T. soy sauce to flavor. Bring to a boil; place shredded pork in casserole and cook for 30 seconds longer. Serve hot.

Diced Pork with Potatoes, Carrots and Green Peppers

Ingredients:

1 lb. boneless pork loin

8 oz. potatoes

8 oz. carrots

1 green pepper

1 T. scallions, chopped

1 t. salt

1 t. sugar

1 1/2 T. soy sauce

Cornstarch

1/2 T. rice wine

Instructions:

1. Dice pork. Peel and dice potatoes and carrots; parboil until almost done. Remove and drain. Cut green pepper open; remove seeds and dice.

2. Mix pork with 1/2 T. soy sauce, rice wine and 1 T. cornstarch.

3. Heat 3 T. oil in wok; when hot, stir-fry pork until color changes. Remove.

4. Heat oil again, then stir-fry green peppers briefly; add potatoes, carrots and pork. Stir-fry to blend flavors. Season with 1/2 T. soy sauce, salt and sugar.

5. Sprinkle scallions over and serve hot.

Stir-Fried Barbecued Pork and Sausage with Chinese Cabbage

Ingredients:

8 oz. Chinese sausage (lup cheong)

8 oz. barbecued pork (char siu)

8 oz. Chinese cabbage, cut in bite-size pieces

1 clove garlic

1/2 t. salt

1/2 T. soy sauce

Instructions:

1. Slice sausage and pork.
2. Parboil Chinese cabbage; remove and drain well.
3. Slice garlic clove.
4. Heat 3 T. oil in wok. When hot, stir-fry garlic until fragrant. Add sausage, barbecued pork and Chinese cabbage to stir-fry. Season with salt and soy sauce; serve hot.

Stuffed Green Peppers

Ingredients:

12 oz. ground pork

3 green peppers

8 oz. shrimp, cleaned and shelled

3-4 dried shrimp

1/2 T. fermented salted soy beans

1 t. chopped ginger

1 T. chopped scallions

Cornstarch

1 t. salt

1 t. sugar

1 1/2 T. soy sauce

Instructions:

1. Soak dried shrimp until soft. Mash dried and fresh shrimp meat, then mix with ground pork. Add 1/2 T. soy sauce, salt, 1/2 T. cornstarch and mix well.

2. Cut each green pepper into 3 parts; dust with cornstarch and fill with ground meat mixture

3. Heat 3 T. oil in a wok; fry stuffed peppers, meat side down until lightly brown. Remove.

4. Heat oil again; add soy beans, garlic and ginger; stir-fry until fragrant. Add green peppers, 1 T. soy sauce, sugar and 1/2 C. water. Simmer for about 5 minutes until gravy is made. Serve hot.

Ham, Pork and Preserved Egg Sausage

Ingredients:

1 pork tripe

1 lb. ham

2 lb. boneless pork loin

3 preserved eggs

3 salted eggs

2 t. salt

1 bottle Shao hsing wine

Instructions:

1. Dice ham, salted egg and preserved eggs and cut pork into small cubes. Blend all with salt.
2. Stuff above ingredients into tripe and sew ends with thread.
3. Place tripe into pot with water to cover; cook over low heat for 1 hour. Remove.
4. Soak in Shao hsing wine; put into refrigerator after cooled.
5. Slice and serve.

Pork Rolls

Ingredients:

1 lb. ground pork

3-4 water chestnuts

8 oz. shrimp, shelled and cleaned

3 dried mushrooms

8 eggroll skins

3 scallions, sliced

1 1/2 t. salt

1 t. sugar

Cornstarch

1 1/2 T. soy sauce

Instructions:

1. Mince water chestnuts and shrimp.
2. Mix pork with water chestnuts and shrimp; add 1 t. salt, sugar and 1 t. cornstarch. Mix well.
3. Spread small amount of pork mixture on each skin; wrap as for spring rolls; fasten with toothpick.
4. Heat 1 T. oil in wok; stir-fry scallions until fragrant. Add 3 C. water, dried mushrooms, pork rolls, soy sauce, 1/2 t. salt, sugar, and bring to boil. Reduce heat and simmer for 40 minutes.

Stir-Fried Liver and Sugar Snap Peas

Ingredients:

1 lb. liver

8 oz. sugar snap peas

1 t. chopped ginger

3 stalks green onion, 2" sections

1 t. salt

1 t. sugar

1/2 T. rice wine

Instructions:

1. Slice liver; mix with chopped ginger, rice wine, soy sauce and 1/2 T. cornstarch.
2. Heat 3 T. oil in wok; when hot, stir-fry green onion until fragrant. Add sugar snap peas and stir-fry briefly. Remove.
3. Heat remaining oil; stir-fry liver until almost done. Add scallions and peas; season with salt and sugar. Serve hot.

Kidneys with Sesame Oil

Ingredients:

2 pork kidneys

1/2 C. black sesame oil

5 slices ginger

1 1/2 t. salt

1/2 C. rice wine

Instructions:

1. Prepare kidneys--cut open, remove white sinews, and cut into bite-sized pieces. Score surface.

2. Heat sesame oil in wok; when hot, stir-fry ginger until fragrant. Add kidney pieces and stir-fry.

3. Add 1/2 C. rice wine and 1/2 C. water; bring to a boil and season with salt. Serve hot.

Pork and Vegetable Croquettes

Ingredients:

3/4 lb. ground pork

1 lb. potatoes

8 oz. carrots

1 onion

2 t. salt

1 t. sugar

Cornstarch

Flour

Instructions:

1. Peel potatoes, boil in water until tender. Remove, drain and mash. Dice onions and carrots; cook carrots in boiling water until tender.

2. Mix well ground pork, mashed potatoes, carrot, onions, salt, sugar and 1 T. cornstarch. Roll into balls and pat flat to form patties.

3. Dip in beaten egg and then flour. Pour oil into wok; heat. When hot, deep-fry patties over medium heat until golden brown. Serve hot.

Shredded Beef with Mushrooms

Ingredients:

5 dried mushrooms

8 oz. straw mushrooms

1 1/4 lb. beef

3 stalks green onion, 1" slices

1 t. salt

1 t. sugar

2 T. soy sauce

1/2 T. rice wine

Instructions:

1. Soak dried mushrooms until tender; cut off stems and shred. Cut off roots of straw mushrooms.
2. Shred beef; mix with soy sauce, rice wine and 1 t. cornstarch. Let marinate briefly.
3. Heat 4 T. oil in wok; when hot, add beef and stir-fry until color changes. Remove from wok.
4. Stir-fry dried mushrooms and straw mushrooms. Add green onions, salt and sugar, then add beef and stir to mix well. Serve hot.

Beef with Oyster Sauce

Ingredients:

1 1/4 lb. beef

10 oz. spinach

3 stalks green onion, 1" slices

1 T. oyster sauce

1/2 t. salt

1/2 T. rice wine

Cornstarch

Instructions:

1. Cut beef into slivers; blend well with oyster sauce, rice wine and 1 t. cornstarch.
2. Heat 2 T. oil in wok; when hot, stir-fry spinach.
3. Heat 3 T. oil in wok; when hot, stir-fry green onions until fragrant. Add beef and stir-fry evenly. Remove and arrange over spinach. Serve hot.

Stir-Fried Beef with Onions and Ginger

Ingredients:

1 1/2 lb. beef

6 slices ginger

6 scallions, 1" slices

1/2 t. salt

1 T. soy sauce

1/2 T. oyster sauce

1/2 T. rice wine

Cornstarch

Instructions:

1. Slice beef thinly; add salt, rice wine, 1 t. cornstarch and soy sauce. Mix well.
2. Heat 2 T. oil in wok; when hot, stir-fry beef until color changes. Add oyster sauce, mix well and remove.
3. Heat remaining oil in wok; stir-fry scallions and ginger until fragrant. Add beef to mix flavors. Serve hot.

Braised Beef and Turnips

Ingredients:

1 lb. shank beef

1 lb. turnips

3 scallions, 1" sections

3 slices ginger

1/2 t. salt

1 t. sugar

1/2 T. rice wine

3 T. soy sauce

Instructions:

1. Peel turnips; cut into cubes. Cut beef into cubes and mix with 1 T. rice wine and 1 T. soy sauce.
2. Heat 3 T. oil in wok; when hot, stir-fry scallions and ginger until fragrant. Add beef and stir-fry until color changes.
3. Add 5 C. water, turnips and 2 T. soy sauce. Bring to boil then reduce heat. Simmer for 1 1/2 hours and flavor with salt and sugar. Remove to ceramic casserole and cook over high heat for 1 minute.

Meatballs and Tofu

Ingredients:

1 lb. ground beef

2 cubes bean curd/tofu

2-3 carrots and bamboo shoots

4 baby bok choy

5 straw mushrooms

3 scallions, 1" slices

1 t. salt

1 t. sugar

1 1/2 t. soy sauce

Cornstarch, sesame oil and black pepper

Instructions:

1. Mix ground beef with 1/2 t. salt and 1 t. cornstarch. Form small meatballs; cook in boiling water until done.
2. Cut bean curd into bite-sized pieces. Peel and slice bamboo shoots and carrots. Halve baby bok choy.
3. Heat 3 T. oil in wok; when hot, stir-fry scallions until fragrant. Add bamboo shoots, carrots, mushrooms and bok choy and stir-fry briefly.
4. Add 2 C. water, 1/2 t. salt, sugar, soy sauce, meatballs and tofu. Stew for 15 minutes; thicken with cornstarch/water solution. Sprinkle with pepper and sesame oil; serve hot.

Stir-Fried Tripe and Green Peppers

Ingredients:

1 piece tripe

2 green peppers

1/2 T. fermented and salted black beans

2 slices ginger

3 stalks scallions, 1" pieces

2 cloves garlic

1 T. bean sauce

1 t. sugar

1/2 T. soy sauce

1/2 T. rice wine

Instructions:

1. Rub tripe with cornstarch; rinse and slice. Place in hot water and boil. When tender, remove, drain, and slice.
2. Cut open green peppers; remove seeds and stem. Cut into pieces.
3. Heat 3 T. oil in wok; when hot stir fry green peppers until fragrant and remove.
4. Heat remaining oil and add fermented beans, ginger, scallions, garlic and bean sauce until fragrant.
5. Add sliced tripe and stir-fry briefly. Add green peppers; mix well and season with sugar, rice wine and soy sauce.

Shrimp-Stuffed Chicken Breast

Ingredients:

1 lb. shrimp, peeled and cleaned

1 lb. chicken breast

2 t. salt

1/2 T. rice wine

Cornstarch

Black pepper

Instructions:

1. Mash shrimp meat; mix with 1 t. salt, rice wine, some black pepper and 1 t. cornstarch.
2. Sprinkle 1 t. salt on chicken breast; let stand for 10 minutes.
3. Dust chicken breast with cornstarch; spread shrimp on breast meat and fold breast in half; enclosing mixture within.
4. Heat oil in wok; when hot, add chicken breast and fry over medium heat until golden brown.
5. Remove, drain and slice to serve.

Braised Chicken with Mushrooms

Ingredients:

1 whole chicken

2 2/3 oz. dried mushrooms (like shiitake)

2 scallions

1/2 oz. ginger

1/3 cup of cooking wine

1/2 oz. almonds

1/2 oz. loquat (cut into sm. pieces)

1 small bamboo shoot

Chinese napa (or any type of Chinese green)

Instructions:

1. Clean chicken, scald in boiling water for 15 minutes.
2. Soak mushrooms, remove stalks.
3. Chop scallions, slice ginger and bamboo.
4. Place chicken, mushrooms, scallions, ginger, bamboo, almonds, Chinese greens and loquat in a large cooking pot, add 12 cups of boiled water and the cooking wine, cook over medium heat for about 30 minutes. Remove excess fat, reduce heat and braise for 2 hours. Keep chicken continuously soaked in liquid; adding boiling water if necessary.
5. Remove chicken and mushrooms and place in a serving dish. Pour soup and rest of ingredients over chicken and mushrooms and serve.

Steamed Cellophane-Wrapped Chicken

Ingredients:

2 chicken thighs

3 stalks scallion, 1" sections

2 slices ginger

2 T. soy sauce

1 t. sugar

1/2 T. rice wine

1 T. hot bean paste

1/2 C. flour

Instructions:

1. Bone and cut thigh meat into chunks. Mix with sliced ginger, scallions, soy sauce, sugar, hot bean paste and rice wine; add flour to mix well.

2. Cut cellophane into 2 inch squares; place one or two chunks of chicken on cellophane and wrap as for egg rolls.

3. Bring water in steamer to boil; place wrapped chicken in steamer basket and steam for 30 minutes.

Steamed Chicken and Mushrooms

Ingredients:

2 chicken thighs

6 dried mushrooms (like shiitake)

3 scallions, 1" sections

1 t. salt

1 t. sugar

2 T. soy sauce

1/2 T. rice wine

Cornstarch

Instructions:

1. Chop thighs into chunks. Mix well with scallions, salt, sugar, soy sauce, rice wine and 1 t. cornstarch.
2. Soak dried mushrooms to soften; drain and cut off stems.
3. Blend chicken with mushrooms; place in steamer to steam for 15 minutes.

Braised Chicken and Onions

Ingredients:

2 chicken thighs

5 small pearl onions

3 slices ginger

1/2 t. salt

1 t. sugar

1/2 T. rice wine

2 T. soy sauce

Cornstarch

Instructions:

1. Chop thighs into bite-sized pieces. Mix well with salt, sugar, rice wine, soy sauce and 1 t. cornstarch.
2. Heat 3 T. oil in wok and stir-fry onions and ginger slices. Add chicken and brown. Add 1/2 C. water and braise for 10 minutes.
3. Add 1/2 T. oil into ceramic pot; heat and put chicken into pot. Cover with lid and simmer for several minutes. Serve hot.

Stir-Fried Chicken with Black Pepper

Ingredients:

1 lb. boneless chicken breast

1 onion

2 carrots

1 t. chopped garlic

1 t. each salt and sugar

2 T. soy sauce

1/2 T. rice wine

Cornstarch

1/2 T. black pepper

Instructions:

1. Peel and slice onion. Peel and shred carrots.
2. Sliver chicken add garlic, salt, sugar, soy sauce, rice wine, 1 t. cornstarch and pepper to mix well.
3. Heat 1 T. oil in wok; stir-fry onions and carrots until limp. Remove.
4. Add 3 T. oil to wok; heat and stir-fry chicken until almost done. Add onions and carrots; mix well and serve hot.

Chicken and Walnuts

Ingredients:

1 lb. boneless chicken breast

1 C. walnuts

1 stalk celery

1 T. chopped scallions

1 t. salt

1 t. sugar

1 T. soy sauce

Cornstarch

Instructions:

1. Soak walnuts in sugar/water solution 4 hours. Remove, drain, and dry well. Fry in moderately hot oil until golden brown. Remove and drain.

2. Dice celery. Cut chicken into cubes and mix with scallions, salt, sugar, soy sauce and 1 t. cornstarch.

3. Heat 3 T. oil in wok; when hot, add diced chicken and stir-fry until almost done. Add celery and walnuts; stir-fry to mix well and serve hot.

Stir-Fried Chicken with Celery and Jellyfish

Ingredients:

1 lb. boneless chicken breast

8 oz. jellyfish

2 stalks celery

1/2 t. chopped ginger

1 T. chopped scallions

1 t. salt

1 T. soy sauce

1/2 T. rice wine

Cornstarch

Instructions:

1. Cut celery into strips. Shred jellyfish and chicken breast; add ginger, scallions, 1/2 T. soy sauce; cornstarch and rice wine to mix.

2. Heat 3 T. oil in wok; stir-fry shredded chicken until almost dome. Add jellyfish gradually, then celery to stir-fry. Season with salt and 1/2 T. soy sauce; mix well and serve hot.

Stir-Fried Giblets with Celery

Ingredients:

1 lb. gizzards

2 stalks celery, sliced diagonally

1 t. chopped ginger

1 t. salt

1 t. sugar

1/2 T. rice wine

Cornstarch

Instructions:

1. Remove "skin" from gizzards; cut into chunks. Blanch in boiling water; remove and dry well.
2. Heat 2 T. oil in wok; stir-fry ginger until fragrant. Add gizzard chunks and celery to stir-fry.
3. Add salt, sugar, soy sauce and rice wine. Mix well and thicken with cornstarch/water solution. Serve hot.

Stewed Giblets and Liver

Ingredients:

3/4 lb. chicken gizzards

3/4 lb. chicken liver

3 slices ginger

3 stalks scallion, 1" slices

1/2 T. rice wine

2 t. soy sauce

Black pepper

Instructions:

1. Remove "skin" from gizzards; marinate gizzards and livers with ginger, scallions and rice wine briefly. Remove and drain well.
2. Heat oil in wok; deep-fry gizzards and liver until done. Remove and drain.
3. Sprinkle with black pepper; re-heat 2 T. oil in wok and add gizzards and liver. Stir-fry over high heat until golden. Serve hot.

Stir-Fried Frog and Garlic

Ingredients:

3 pairs of frogs legs

10 garlic cloves

3 stalks scallions, 1" slice

3 slices ginger

1 t. salt

1 t. sugar

1 1/2 T. soy sauce

1/2 T. rice wine

Cornstarch

Instructions:

1. Cut frogs legs into chunks. Blend with salt, sugar, soy sauce, rice wine and 1 t. cornstarch.
2. Heat 1 C. oil in wok; deep-fry garlic cloves until golden. Remove. Quick-fry scallions and ginger with remaining oil. Add frogs legs and garlic to stir-fry evenly.
3. Place in casserole and cook over high heat for 1 more minute. Serve hot.

Colorful Shredded Duck

Ingredients:

Half a roast duck

2-3 carrots

2-3 onions

2-3 green peppers

1 red chile pepper

1 t. sugar

1/2 t. salt

Instructions:

1. Bone duck; shred meat. Peel and cut carrots, onions, green peppers and chile pepper in slivers.
2. Heat 2 T. oil in wok; stir-fry onions until fragrant.
3. Gradually add carrots, green peppers, red chile pepper, and duck meat to stir-fry until done.
4. Season with salt and sugar; serve hot.

Braised Curry Duck

Ingredients:

Half a duck

1 onion

1 carrot

2 potatoes

1 C. coconut milk

3 slices ginger

1 t. each salt and sugar

2 T. soy sauce

Cornstarch

1 T. curry powder

Instructions:

1. Cut duck into chunks. Peel onion, carrot and potatoes; cut into chunks.
2. Blend duck with 1 T. soy sauce, rice wine and 1 t. cornstarch.
3. Heat 3 T. oil in wok; stir-fry onions, ginger and curry powder until fragrant.
4. Add duck and stir-fry. When lightly browned, add 5 C. water, 1 T. soy sauce, salt and sugar. Bring to boil and reduce heat. Simmer for 10 minutes until almost done.
5. Add potato, carrot and coconut milk; cook for 15 minutes.
6. Remove to casserole and cook over high heat for one minute. Serve hot.

Braised Duck with Bamboo Shoots and Mushrooms

Ingredients:

Half a duck

8 oz. dried mushrooms (like shiitake)

1/2 C. preserved dried cabbage

3 slices ginger

3 stalks scallions, 1" lengths

1/2 t. salt

1 t. sugar

2 T. soy sauce

1 T. rice wine

Cornstarch

Bamboo shoots

Instructions:

1. Chop duck into chunks; marinate with 1 T. each rice wine and soy sauce and 1 t. cornstarch.
2. Cut bamboo shoots into chunks; soak mushrooms until tender and remove stems.
3. Heat 1/2 C. oil in wok; stir-fry scallions and ginger until fragrant. Add duck and stir-fry until lightly browned.
4. Add 5 C. water, mushrooms, bamboo shoots, preserved dried cabbage and 1 T. soy sauce. Bring to a boil; reduce heat and simmer until duck is tender. Season with salt and sugar; serve hot.

Braised Goose and Plums

Ingredients:

Half a goose

10 plums

3 slices ginger

3 scallions, 1" slices

1 t. salt

1 t. sugar

2 T. soy sauce

1 T. rice wine

Cornstarch

Instructions:

1. Chop goose; marinate with 1 T. soy sauce, rice wine and 1 t. cornstarch. Pit plums, cut into pieces.
2. Heat 1/2 C. oil in wok; stir-fry scallions and ginger until fragrant.
3. Add goose meat and stir-fry. Add 5 C. water, plums and 1 T. soy sauce. Bring to a boil, reduce heat and simmer until goose is tender.
4. Add salt and sugar; continue to simmer for 15 minutes. Serve hot.

Boiled Goose

Ingredients:

1 lb. goose intestines

8 oz. bean sprouts

2 Chinese chives

2 t. salt

Instructions:

1. Remove stems of bean sprouts; cut chives into sections.
2. Place goose intestines, bean sprouts and chives in boiling water until well done. Serve with sauce below.

Sauce:

Blend 1/2 T. soy sauce, 1 T. sweet and hot sauce, 1/2 T. minced garlic, and 1/2 T. ginger sauce; mix well. May also use hot mustard sauce.

Sweet and Sour Fish

Ingredients:

1 whole fish, scaled and cleaned (yellow croaker, bass, etc.)

2-3 green peppers

2-3 red chiles

2-3 onions

3 stalks scallions, 1" slices

1 t. salt

1/2 T. rice wine

1 t. sugar

1/2 T. vinegar

3 T. ketchup

Flour

Instructions:

1. Make 3-4 diagonal slashes on each side of fish. Marinate with salt and rice wine.
2. Slice green peppers, chiles, onions and scallions.
3. Dust fish with flour; place in hot oil to deep fry until golden. Remove and place on serving platter.
4. Heat 3 T. oil in wok; stir-fry chiles, green peppers, scallions and onions until fragrant.
5. Add ketchup, sugar, vinegar and small amount of water; stir-fry evenly. Remove and pour over fish to serve.

Steamed Whole Fish with Black Beans

Ingredients:

1 whole fish, scaled and cleaned (flounder, bass, etc.)

1/2 T. fermented black beans

3 slices ginger

5 stalks scallions, sliced 1" sections

1/2 t. sugar

1 t. salt

1/2 T. rice wine

1/2 T. soy sauce

Cornstarch

Instructions:

1. Make 3-4 slashes on each side of fish; marinate with salt and rice wine.
2. Mash fermented beans; stir-fry in wok until fragrant.
3. Slice scallions and shred onions.
4. Place sliced scallions and ginger on steam proof platter; place fish on top. Sprinkle with fermented beans.
5. Place fish in steamer with water at vigorous boil for 5 minutes. Remove and drain liquid, reserving it.
6. Heat 1 T. oil, add shredded scallions and stir-fry evenly; sprinkle in fish.
7. Heat liquid from fish, soy sauce and sugar until boiling, thicken with cornstarch/water solution; pour over fish and serve.

Stir-Fried Fish and Vegetables

Ingredients:

1 lb. white-meat fish fillets (cod, halibut, etc.)

3 dried mushrooms

2-3 carrots

2-3 bamboo shoots

2-3 stalks celery

3 stalks scallions, sliced

2 slices ginger

1 1/2 t. salt

1 T. soy sauce

1/2 T. rice wine

Cornstarch

Black pepper

Instructions:

1. Cut fish into chunks; marinate with rice wine, 1 t. salt, 1 t. cornstarch and dash of pepper.
2. Soak mushrooms to soften and cut off stems. Shred mushrooms.
3. Peel carrots; slice carrots, bamboo shoots and celery.
4. Heat 2 C. oil in wok; deep-fry fish until done. Remove and drain.
5. Heat 2 T. oil in pan; stir-fry scallions and ginger until fragrant. Add mushrooms, carrots, bamboo shoots, fish and celery; stir-fry evenly. Flavor with 1/2 t. salt and soy sauce; serve hot.

Fried Fish and Pineapple

Ingredients:

1 whole fish, cleaned and scaled (grouper, bass, etc.)

1 small can pineapple slices

2 green peppers

2-3 red chiles

1/2 C. preserved ginger

1 1/2 t. salt

Cornstarch

Black pepper

Instructions:

1. Cut fish into chunks. Cut pineapple slices into chunks. Cut peppers (both red and green) into pieces.
2. Marinate fish with dash of pepper, 1 t. cornstarch, rice wine and 1 t. salt.
3. Heat 2 C. oil in wok; deep-fry fish until done. Remove and drain.
4. Heat 1 T. oil in pan; stir-fry peppers and ginger until fragrant. Add fish and pineapple chunks; stir-fry evenly. Season with 1/2 t. salt and serve hot.

魚

Stir-Fried Eel and Chives

Ingredients:

1 lb. eels

8 oz. chives

1/2 T. chopped garlic

1 t. chopped ginger

1 t. sugar

1 t. salt

1/2 T. rice wine

2 T. soy sauce

Cornstarch

Black Pepper

Instructions:

1. Wash eels and blanch in boiling water. Remove and slice thinly. Marinate with ginger, 1/2 t. salt, sugar, rice wine, soy sauce and 1 t. cornstarch.
2. Slice chives.
3. Heat 2 T. oil in wok; stir-fry chives until soft; season with 1/2 t. salt and remove to serving dish.
4. Heat 1/2 C. oil in pan; stir-fry garlic until fragrant; stir-fry eels until done. Season with pepper and thicken with cornstarch/water solution. Place on chives and serve.

Braised Fish

Ingredients:

1 large fish head (carp, grouper, etc.)

8 oz. sheet jelly (Hun Pi)

8 oz. lean boneless pork

10 garlic cloves

3 slices ginger

3 onions, sliced

1 t. salt

1 T. rice wine

2 T. soy sauce

Flour

Instructions:

1. Slice pork; add 1/2 t. soy sauce to mix well. Cut sheet jelly into long narrow pieces.
2. Dust fish head with flour; fry in hot oil until golden. Remove and drain.
3. Heat 3 T. oil; stir-fry garlic until golden and remove.
4. Stir-fry pork; add fish head, garlic and sheet jelly.
5. Flavor with salt and rice wine; remove to casserole and braise for 2 more minutes. Serve hot.

Stir-Fried Shrimp and Vegetables

Ingredients:

1 lb. shrimp, cleaned and peeled

4 pieces of bacon

8 oz. bamboo shoots

8 oz. asparagus

2 stalks scallions, 1" slices

1 t. chopped ginger

1 t. salt

1/2 T. rice wine

Cornstarch

Instructions:

1. Slash along spine of each shrimp so shrimp will curl into ball when cooked. Cut bacon into 1 1/2 inch pieces.
2. Slice asparagus and bamboo shoots.
3. Blend shrimp with ginger, rice wine and 1 t. cornstarch.
4. Heat 3 T. oil in wok; stir-fry shrimp and bacon until almost done. Remove and drain.
5. Stir-fry scallion sections in remaining oil until fragrant. Add shrimp, bacon and bamboo shoots; stir-fry and season with salt. Serve hot.

Fried Shrimp

Ingredients:

1 lb. shrimp, cleaned and peeled (with tail shell left on)

1 t. salt

1 t. sugar

1/2 T. rice wine

2 eggs

1 C. flour

Bread crumbs (panko-type)

Instructions:

1. Slash along spine of shrimp. Marinate in salt, sugar and rice wine.
2. Beat eggs. Dust shrimp with flour; dip in beaten eggs and then in bread crumbs.
3. Deep-fry in wok with hot oil until golden brown. Remove and drain to serve.

Shrimp with Barbecue Sauce

Ingredients:

1 lb. shrimp, shells and head intact

3 stalks scallions, 1" sections

3 slices ginger

1/2 T. chopped garlic

1/2 T. chopped red chile

1 T. barbecue sauce

1 t. salt

1 t. sugar

1/2 T. rice wine

Instructions:

1. Marinate the shrimp in salt, rice wine and sugar.
2. Heat 3 C. oil in wok; deep-fry shrimp until they change color. Remove and drain.
3. Heat 1 T. oil in pan; stir-fry garlic, red chile, scallions, ginger and barbecue sauce. Add shrimp and stir-fry to mix flavors. Serve hot.

Stir-Fried Scallops and Baby Bok Choy

Ingredients:

1 1/2 lb. scallops

4 baby bok choy

1 T. chopped garlic

1 t. chopped ginger

1 t. sugar

1/2 T. vinegar

3 T. ketchup

Instructions:

1. Blanch scallops in boiling water; remove and drain. Blanch baby bok choy in boiling water; remove, drain, cut in half and arrange on serving platter.
2. Heat 2 T. oil in wok; stir-fry garlic and ginger until fragrant. Add ketchup, sugar, vinegar and 1/4 C. water to mix well.
3. Add scallops and stir-fry. When done, pour over bok choy and serve.

Stir-Fried Squid with Shrimp Paste

Ingredients:

1 lb. squid

1 cucumber

1 carrot

3 scallions, 1" slices

1 t. sugar

1/2 T. rice wine

1/2 T. shrimp paste

Instructions:

1. Clean squid; score surface and cut into bite-sized pieces. Blanch squid in boiling water; remove and drain.

2. Slice cucumber, carrots and then cut carrots decoratively into flower or star shapes.

3. Heat 2 T. oil in wok; stir-fry scallions and shrimp paste until fragrant.

4. Add carrots, cucumber and squid to stir-fry; season with sugar and rice wine and then thicken with cornstarch/ water solution. Serve hot.

* Note: Shrimp paste is salty; hence extra salt is unnecessary.

Braised Oyster with Garlic and Bean Curd

Ingredients:

8 oz. oysters, shucked

4 oz. bean curd

8 oz. lean pork or beef

2 stalks scallions, 1" slices

5 cloves garlic

1 t. salt

1 t. sugar

1/2 T. rice wine

1 1/2 T. soy sauce

Instructions:

1. Cut bean curd; deep-fry in hot oil until golden. Remove and drain.
2. Slice meat thinly; add 1/2 T. soy sauce to stir evenly.
3. Heat 2 T. oil in wok; stir-fry scallions until fragrant. Add meat and stir-fry until color changes.
4. Add 2 C. water and 1 T. soy sauce; bring to a boil and cook over medium heat for 10 minutes.
5. Season with salt and sugar; add oysters and cook until done. Thicken with corn-starch/water mixture. Remove to casserole and cook for 1 minute; serve hot.

Stir-Fried Crabs with Seafood Sauce

Ingredients:

5 crabs

5 stalks scallions, 1" slices

3 slices ginger

1 T. Hoisin sauce (plum sauce)

1 C. flour

Instructions:

1. Cut crabs into chunks; discard legs. Deep-fry crabs in hot oil until golden brown; remove and drain.

2. Heat 2 T. oil in wok; stir-fry ginger and scallions until fragrant. Add Hoisin sauce, stir, and add crab pieces. Stir-fry to mix well and serve hot.

*Note: Hoisin sauce is a condiment in itself; no other seasonings are necessary.

Braised Crab with Scallion and Ginger

Ingredients:

2 crabs

5 stalks scallion, 1" slices

5 slices ginger

1 C. chicken stock

Instructions:

1. Steam crabs for 3 minutes. Remove and cut into 4 pieces.
2. Heat 2 T. oil in wok; stir-fry scallions and ginger until fragrant. Add crabs to stir-fry.
3. Pour stock into wok and simmer until gravy is reduced. Serve hot.

*Note: Stock may also be a combination of chicken and ham stock.

Sautéed Tremella with Peppers and Pineapple

Ingredients:

2 oz. tremella (yellow fungi)

2 green peppers

2 red chiles

4 slices pineapple

1 t. sugar

1/2 T. vinegar

1 T. ketchup

Instructions:

1. Soak tremella in water until it expands. Blanch in boiling water and remove.
2. Slice green peppers, chiles and pineapple into chunks.
3. Heat 1 T. oil in wok; stir-fry green peppers and chiles until fragrant.
4. Heat 1 T. oil into pan; add ketchup, sugar and vinegar to mix evenly. Add tremella, green peppers, chiles and pineapple, stir-frying to mix well. Serve hot.

Braised Mushrooms

Ingredients:

8 dried shiitake mushrooms

8 oz. straw mushrooms

8 oz. button mushrooms

5 baby bok choy

1 T. soy sauce

1 t. salt

1 t. sugar

Sesame oil

3 C. chicken stock

Instructions:

1. Soak shiitake mushrooms in water until tender; remove stems. Add salt, sugar and soy sauce to soaking water and bring to boil; cook mushrooms until most of liquid is absorbed. Remove and place on serving platter.
2. Bring stock to boil; add fresh and straw mushrooms and cook briefly. Remove and place on serving dish.
3. Cut bok choy in half; blanch in boiling stock, remove and place on serving dish also.
4. Discard stock save 1 T.; thicken with cornstarch/water solution. Add a few drops sesame oil and then pour over mushrooms and bok choy to serve.

Sweet and Sour Lotus Roots

Ingredients:

1 lb. lotus roots

2 green peppers

2 red chiles

1 t. salt

2 t. sugar

1 T. vinegar

Instructions:

1. Peel and rinse lotus root; slice in matchstick form. Slice green peppers and red chiles similarly.
2. Heat 2 T. oil in wok; stir-fry peppers and chiles until fragrant. Remove.
3. Stir-fry lotus roots in remaining oil until done. Add green peppers and chiles to stir-fry evenly.
4. Season with salt, sugar and vinegar.

Baby Corn with Green and White Asparagus

Ingredients:

8 oz. green asparagus

8 oz. white asparagus

8 oz. baby corn

1 C. milk

1 T. coconut milk

2 t. sugar

Cornstarch

Instructions:

1. Blanch vegetables in boiling water. Remove and drain. Arrange on serving dish.
2. Heat milk, coconut milk and sugar until almost boiling. Thicken with cornstarch/water solution. Pour over vegetables and serve.

Bean Curd and Shrimp Patties

Ingredients:

8 oz. shrimp, cleaned and shelled

2 blocks bean curd

4 baby bok choy

1 1/2 t. salt

1 t. sugar

Black pepper

1 C. chicken stock

1/2 T. soy sauce

Instructions:

1. Steam bean curd for 3 minutes. Remove and press out water in towel. Mash bean curd.
2. Mash shrimp and blend with bean curd, salt, sugar and dash of pepper. Shape into patties; dust with cornstarch and deep-fry in hot oil until golden brown.
3. Halve bok choy; blanch in boiling stock. Drain and place on serving platter.
4. Bring soy sauce to boil with 1/2 C. stock.; thicken with cornstarch/water mixture. Arrange patties atop bok choy and pour gravy over. Serve hot.

Mustard Greens with Crab

Ingredients:

1 crab or 4 oz. crab meat

1 lb. mustard green

3 C. chicken stock

Cornstarch

Black pepper

Instructions:

1. Slice mustard greens into bite-sized pieces; blanch in boiling water. Remove, drain and place in serving dish.
2. Cook crab in boiling water; remove and shell, saving meat (skip this step in the case of crab meat.).
3. Bring 1 C. stock to boil; add crab meat. Thicken with cornstarch/water solution; flavor with pepper. Pour over mustard greens and serve.

Sausage and Chives

Ingredients:

4 oz. chives

1 lb. Chinese sausage

1 t. salt

2 t. sugar

1 T. soy sauce

Instructions:

1. Cut chives into 1" sections. Slice sausage into thin strips.
2. Heat 2 T. oil in wok; stir-fry chives until slightly tender. Season with salt and remove.
3. Heat 2 T. oil again; stir-fry sausage and flavor with soy sauce and ginger.
4. Add chives, stir-fry to mix evenly and serve hot.

Boiled Wax Gourd with Vegetables

Ingredients:

1 1/2 lb. wax gourd

1/4 C. corn

3 black mushrooms

1/4 C. tender soybeans, shelled

2 carrots

4-5 small shrimp, shelled

5 C. stock

Sesame oil

Instructions:

1. Peel wax gourd; cut into chunks. Bring stock to boil and add wax gourd; cook until tender. Remove and place in serving dish.

2. Remove stems of black mushrooms; chop mushrooms. Peel carrots and dice. Rinse soybeans.

3. Bring stock to boil again; add vegetables and cook until tender. Thicken with cornstarch/water solution.

4. Sprinkle with a few drops of sesame oil and then pour over wax gourd, stirring to mix well. Serve hot.

Cabbage, Noodles and Fish

Ingredients:

1/4 Chinese cabbage

1 bunch cellophane noodles

1 white-meat, freshwater fish

1 t. salt

Sesame oil

Instructions:

1. Shred cabbage. Soak noodles until soft and then tear into small pieces.
2. Cut fish into small pieces; fry in hot oil.
3. Heat 2 T. oil in wok; stir-fry Chinese cabbage briefly.
4. Add 1 C. water, fish, and salt and bring to boil. Add noodles; cook briefly and sprinkle with sesame oil. Serve hot.

Stir-Fried Carrots and Turnips

Ingredients:

3/4 lb. turnips

3/4 lb. carrots

2 dried black mushrooms (like shiitake)

2 green peppers

1 t. salt

1 t. sugar

Instructions:

1. Soak mushrooms in water until soft; remove stems. Cut into matchstick form.
2. Peel carrots and turnips; cut into matchstick form and blanch in boiling water briefly. Remove and drain.
3. Cut green peppers into matchstick form as well.
4. Heat 2 T. oil in wok; quick-fry green peppers and mushrooms until fragrant.
5. Add carrots and turnips and stir-fry to mix well. Season with salt and sugar; serve hot.

Eggs with Pork and Peas

Ingredients:

12 oz. boneless pork loin

8 oz. peas

4 eggs

1 t. salt

1/2 T. soy sauce

Cornstarch

Instructions:

1. Cube pork; add soy sauce and 1 t. corn-starch and mix well.
2. Blanch peas.
3. Beat eggs and add 1/2 t. salt.
4. Heat 2 T. oil in wok; stir-fry peas briefly. Add 1/2 t. salt to flavor and remove.
5. Heat oil in wok again and stir-fry pork until done. Add peas and eggs to reheat. Serve hot.

*Note: Adding some water to the eggs before cooking will make the eggs some-what more tender.

Sauteed Cauliflower

Ingredients:

1 head cauliflower, cut into florets

1 t. curry

1 C. milk

1 t. salt

1 t. sugar

Cornstarch

Instructions:

1. Blanch cauliflower in boiling water; remove and drain.
2. Heat 2 T. oil in wok; stir-fry cauliflower briefly and remove.
3. Heat remaining oil in wok; quick-fry curry powder until fragrant. Add 1/2 C. water, salt and sugar and bring to boil.
4. Add milk and heat again almost to boil. Thicken with cornstarch/water solution and then pour over cauliflower in serving dish.

Eggplant with Minced Chicken

Ingredients:

8 oz. boneless chicken

1 lb. eggplant

1/2 T. chopped garlic

1 t. salt

1 t. sugar

1 1/2 T. soy sauce

3 red onions, peeled and sliced

Instructions:

1. Mince chicken; add 1/2 T. soy sauce and mix well.
2. Cut eggplant in long strips (if Western eggplant, peel first).
3. Heat 2 T. oil in wok; quick-fry garlic and red onions until fragrant.
4. Add chicken and stir-fry. Remove.
5. Add 3 T. oil in wok and stir-fry eggplant until limp. Add 1 1/2 C. water, 1 T. soy sauce, salt, sugar and chicken. Bring to boil and reduce heat to medium.
6. Simmer until eggplant is tender. Remove to casserole and boil over high heat for one minute. Serve hot.

Dried Bean Curd with Peppers

Ingredients:

1 lb. flavored dried bean curd

1 green pepper

3 red chiles

2 pieces fermented bean curd

2 t. sugar

1/2 t. soy sauce

Instructions:

1. Slice dried bean curd in matchstick form.
2. Seed red chiles and green pepper; cut into matchstick form.
3. Heat 2 T. oil in wok; stir-fry peppers and chile until fragrant. Remove.
4. Add 1 more T. oil to wok; heat and quick-fry fermented bean curd until fragrant. Add dried bean curd, green pepper and red chiles.
5. Stir-fry and season with sugar and soy sauce. Serve hot.

Beef and Tomato Soup

Ingredients:

1 lb. beef shank meat

12 oz. carrots

1 tomato

1 T. chopped scallions

3 stalks scallions, 1" slices

3 slices ginger

1 1/2 T. salt

1/2 T. rice wine

Instructions:

1. Blanch beef in boiling water; remove and cut into chunks.
2. Blanch tomato in boiling water; remove, peel and cut into pieces. Peel carrots and cut into chunks.
3. Bring 5 C. water with beef, tomato, sliced scallions and sliced ginger to boil. Reduce heat and simmer over low heat for 1 hour.
4. Add carrots, salt and rice wine; continue to simmer for 30 minutes. Sprinkle with chopped scallions and serve hot.

Mushroom Chicken Soup

Ingredients:

1/2 chicken

1 oz. dried white fungi

5 dried black mushrooms

3 slices ginger

3 stalks scallions, 1" pieces

1 1/2 t. salt

1/2 T. rice wine

Instructions:

1. Chop chicken into chunks; blanch in boiling water and remove.
2. Soak fungi and black mushrooms until soft. Remove stems of mushrooms.
3. Bring 5 C. water, chicken, fungi, mushrooms, ginger and scallions to boil over high heat. Reduce heat and simmer over low heat for 30 minutes.
4. Remove ginger and scallions; add salt and rice wine to flavor and continue to cook for 15 minutes.
5. Serve hot.

Pork Meatball Soup

Ingredients:

3/4 lb. ground pork

1 lb. cucumber

5 straw mushrooms

2 slices ginger

3 scallions, 1" sections

1 1/2 t. salt

1/2 T. rice wine

Cornstarch

Black pepper

Instructions:

1. Blend pork with 1/2 t. salt, rice wine, 1 t. cornstarch and dash of pepper.
2. Cut cucumber in half lengthwise; remove seeds and cut into chunks.
3. Bring 5 C. water to boil; form pork into little meatballs and add to boiling water to cook.
4. Add cucumber, straw mushrooms, ginger, and scallions; bring to boil and reduce heat. Simmer for 15 minutes; season with 1 t. salt and serve hot.

Sparerib and Taro Soup

Ingredients:

1 lb. spareribs, chopped in 1" pieces

1 lb. taro

3 slices ginger

3 scallions, 1 " slices

1 1/2 t. salt

1/2 T. rice wine

Instructions:

1. Peel taro and cut into chunks. Blanch spareribs in boiling water; remove.
2. Bring 5 C. water, spareribs, ginger and scallions to boil over high heat. Reduce heat and simmer over low heat for 20 minutes.
3. Add taro and cook for 30 minutes more until taro is tender.
4. Season with salt and rice wine; serve hot.

Carp and Vegetable Soup

Ingredients:

1 lb. carp fillets

2 preserved eggs

3 sprays parsley

3 slices ginger

3 stalks scallions, 1" slices

1 1/2 t. salt

1/2 T. rice wine

Black pepper

Sesame oil

Instructions:

1. Slice carp into long narrow strips; marinate in 1/2 t. salt and rice wine.
2. Cut preserved eggs into chunks.
3. Bring 4 C. water, eggs, ginger and scallions to boil. Add carp and parsley; bring to boil again and season with 1 t. salt.
4. Sprinkle with pepper and sesame oil; serve hot.

Roast Duck and Mustard Green Soup

Ingredients:

1/4 roast duck

3/4 lb. mustard green

1 T. minced ginger

1 t. salt

Instructions:

1. Chop roast duck into chunks.
2. Cut mustard greens into small pieces.
3. Bring 4 C. water to boil; add duck and ginger and cook for 15 minutes.
4. Add mustard greens and salt; cook until greens are tender. Serve hot.

Frog and Lotus Seed Soup

Ingredients:

4 pairs frogs legs

8 oz. lotus seeds

3 slices ginger

1 T. rice wine

Black pepper

1 1/2 t. salt

Instructions:

1. Chop frogs legs into chunks and marinate with salt and rice wine.
2. Soak lotus seeds in water.
3. Bring 5 C. water and lotus seeds to boil over high heat. Simmer over low heat for 40 minutes; add ginger and frog pieces and cook until frogs are tender.
4. Flavor with salt and sprinkle with dash of pepper. Serve hot.

Seafood Soup

Ingredients:

1 carp's head

3 oz. shrimp

3 oz. squid

6 oz. clams

5 straw mushrooms

2 each, carrots and bamboo shoots

3 sprays watercress

3 stalks scallions, 1" sections

3 slices ginger

1 1/2 t. salt

1/2 T. rice wine

Instructions:

1. Soak clams in salt solution. Cut squid into chunks Peel carrots and slice. Slice bamboo shoots.
2. Bring 4 C. water to boil; add carp's head, carrots, bamboo shoots, straw mushrooms, scallions and ginger to cook for 20 minutes.
3. Add shrimp, clams, squid and remaining vegetables with salt to flavor.
4. Continue to boil until clams open. Serve hot.

Abalone and Sea Cucumber Soup

Ingredients:

1 canned abalone

1 sea cucumber

2 carrots

2 bamboo shoots

3 oz. snow peas

3 slices ginger

3 scallions, 1" sections

1 1/2 t. salt

1/2 T. rice wine

Instructions:

1. Slice abalone. Clean sea cucumber, remove innards and slice meat.
2. Peel and slice carrots and bamboo shoots. Stem peas.
3. Bring 4 C. water to a boil; add abalone, sea cucumber, carrots, bamboo shoots, ginger and scallions. Cook over moderately high heat for 15 minutes.
4. Add snow peas, salt and rice wine; cook until peas are crispy and tender. Serve hot.

Squid, Noodle and Tender Mustard Green Soup

Ingredients:

12 oz. squid

12 oz. tender mustard greens

1 bunch cellophane noodles

4 C. stock

Instructions:

1. Cut squid into long narrow pieces. Wash mustard greens and mince.
2. Soak noodles until soft.
3. Bring stock to boil; add squid, mustard greens and noodles to boil for 5 minutes.
4. Remove to casserole; bring to boil for 1 minute and serve hot.

Bean Curd and Fish Soup

Ingredients:

1 whole fish (yellow croaker, flounder, bass, etc.)

1 block bean curd

Chinese napa (or any type of Chinese green)

3 slices ginger

1 1/2 t. salt

1/2 T. rice wine

Cornstarch

Black pepper

Instructions:

1. Marinate fish with rice wine and ginger slices. Place in steamer and steam for 3 minutes. Remove and flake fish meat.
2. Cut bean curd into small pieces. Shred Chinese green.
3. Bring 4 C. water to boil; add bean curd, fish and greens. Boil for 3 minutes.
4. Season with salt; thicken with cornstarch/water solution.

Millet and Scallop Soup

Ingredients:

1 can millet

5 dried scallops

1 spray coriander

1/2 t. salt

Black pepper

Instructions:

1. Bring 3 C. water to boil; add millet and shredded dried scallops. Boil for 10 minutes.
2. Season with salt; thicken with cornstarch/water solution.
3. Sprinkle with pepper and chopped coriander. Serve hot.

Beef and Crab Soup

Ingredients:

1 lb. boneless beef

5 straw mushrooms

1 crab

1 spray coriander

1 t. chopped ginger

1/2 T. rice wine

1 1/2 t. salt

Cornstarch

Sesame oil

Instructions:

1. Mince beef; marinate with ginger, salt and rice wine.

2. Mince straw mushrooms and coriander; cook crab and remove meat. (Or use 3 oz. canned crabmeat.)

3. Bring 4 C. water to boil; add beef, mushrooms and crabmeat. Cook over high heat for 10 minutes.

4. Flavor with 1 t. salt; add coriander and thicken with cornstarch/water solution. Sprinkle with sesame oil and serve hot.

Bean Curd and Shrimp Soup

Ingredients:

12 oz. shrimp, shelled and cleaned

3 oz. jingzhen mushrooms

3 black mushrooms

1 stalk celery

1 block bean curd

1 1/2 t. salt

1/2 T. rice wine

Sesame oil

Instructions:

1. Remove stems of mushrooms. Cut bean curd into small pieces.
2. Mince shrimp, black mushrooms and celery.
3. Bring 4 C. water to boil; add shrimp, mushrooms, celery, jingzhen mushrooms and bean curd. Cook over high heat for 10 minutes.
4. Season with salt and rice wine. Thicken with cornstarch/water solution; sprinkle with few drops of sesame oil and serve hot.

It is a fact known throughout the world that the Chinese people love to eat. In particular, they enjoy dining out at restaurants, so it is no surprise that Taiwan's catering trade is so well-developed--or that Taiwan boasts some of the world's finest restaurants.

I have been involved in the catering trade for the past twenty years, and I have always felt that anyone should be able to replicate the dishes prepared by Taiwan's foremost chefs. All they need is a bit of instruction on techniques!

This book, <u>Chinese Cooking--Restaurant Style</u>, is the culmination of one of my fondest hopes--the introduction of the craft of the master chef to the masses. Mixing the ingredients, cutting techniques, duration and degree of heat, cooking--all of these concepts are presented herein so that the average home cook can create fantastic dishes for family and guests.

I hope that all who read this book will profit by it, learning to carry on the delicious tradition of Chinese cooking.

Liang Zhiheng
Chef, Fulinman Restaurant, Huanya Grand Hotel